Practical Home Handbook

# Napkins
## & Napkin Folding

Practical Home Handbook

# Napkins

# & Napkin Folding

Bridget Jones and Madeleine Brehaut

LORENZ BOOKS

This edition is published by Lorenz Books

Lorenz Books is an imprint of Anness Publishing Ltd
Hermes House, 88–89 Blackfriars Road, London SE1 8HA
tel. 020 7401 2077; fax 020 7633 9499

www.lorenzbooks.com
info@anness.com
© Anness Publishing Ltd 1994, 2002

Published in the USA by Lorenz Books,
Anness Publishing Inc.
fax 212 807 6813

This edition distributed in the USA by
National Book Network
tel. 301 459 3366; fax 301 459 1705;

Published in Australia by Lorenz Books,
Anness Publishing Pty Ltd
tel. (02) 8920 8622; fax (02) 8920 8633

This edition distributed in Canada by
General Publishing
tel. 416 445 3333; fax 416 445 5991;

This edition distributed in the UK by
Aurum Press Ltd
tel. 020 7637 3225; fax 020 7580 2469

This edition distributed in New Zealand by
David Bateman Ltd
tel. (09) 415 7664; fax (09) 415 889

A CIP catalogue record for this book is available from the British Library.

*Editorial Director:* Joanna Lorenz
*Project Editor:* Jennifer Jones
*Assistant Editor:* Charles Moxham
*Designer:* Adrian Morris
*Special photography:* James Duncan
*Stylist:* Madeleine Brehaut
*Illustrator:* Kate Simunek

1 3 5 7 9 10 8 6 4 2

# CONTENTS

# NAPKIN ART

*C*risp, *freshly laundered napkins are an essential feature of every well-set table. They may be pressed in large, plain squares and laid at each place with the minimum of fuss and for the maximum effect. Alternatively, they may be* *folded in a variety of ways to complement the food, table layout and occasion. Try some of the ideas in the followi* *pages and use them as a source of inspiration for developi* *your own individual napkin art.*

## PERFECT NAPKINS

Regardless of the simplicity of the meal, fabric napkins must be spotlessly clean and well pressed.

❖ Plain white linen napkins may be embroidered by hand or by machine with a monogram of your initials. This may be surrounded by a wreath of leaves or some other decorative embroidery. Fold monogrammed napkins very simply to display the embroidery.

❖ Press embroidered napkins on the wrong side to make the pattern stand out attractively.

❖ Decorative napkins, trimmed w embroidery or lace or with a prom ent self pattern, should be folded v simply; plain fabric napkins or th with a small decorative border more suitable for elaborate folding.

## NAPKINS FOR BUFFETS

If you are preparing a buffet for comparatively small number, that under fifteen guests, then it is a go idea to use linen napkins if possib The fabrics do not have to be the sa and a virtue can be made of th differences by combining contrasti colours or patterns in an attracti arrangement.

❖ For larger gatherings or when th are lots of children around, it is advantage to have lots of spare pap napkins to deal with any spills. Bear mind that guests rarely retain th napkins after the main course a many may take a second for dessert

❖ Elaborate folding methods are n used for buffet presentation as t emphasis is mainly on the practicalit of carrying a plate, napkin and cutle (flatware). There are a number of stan dard options for placing napkins.

❖ Roll a knife and fork in a napkin. the number of guests is small and spa on the buffet table limited, the cutle and napkins may be fanned out attra tively, near the plates. It is often mo practical to pile them in a basket, two, and place them near the plates on a separate side table with cond ments or bread. Do not roll cutlery fo

### Paper Napkins

Paper napkins are more practical than fabric ones for parties. Choose those that are large, absorbent and fairly thick; the thin, small paper napkins that disintegrate easily are more hindrance than help. The exception to this rule is Japanese paper napkins.

**BRIGHT PAPER NAPKINS** For fun parties use a selection of different coloured paper napkins: pastels or primary colours both work well. Fold them in half, then overlap them in a large basket and fold one napkin into a water lily shape for the centre of the arrangement.

Paper napkins are a practical option for informal barbecues, especially when sticky spareribs and other finger foods are served. When laying a garden table, allow two or three different coloured napkins for each place setting. They may be fanned out simply or pairs of contrasting colours used double for folding shapes such as a water lily or roll-top design.

**JAPANESE PAPER NAPKINS** Look out for fine paper napkins which are very thin but quite strong. They are often delicately patterned and may be round or square, with fluted or gilded edges. As well as being used on their own, they may be used in conjunction with linen napkins for courses which are eaten with the fingers as part of a formal meal, especially when finger bowls are provided. Fold them attractively with the linen napkins, then clear the paper napkins away after they have been used.

*A tartan bow holds a neatly rolled napkin and spoon for a dessert course.*

...essert in the napkin; this should be ...fered separately.

❖ Stack a napkin on each plate.

❖ Fold the napkins in half diagonally ...o make triangles and overlap these on ...ne side of the buffet table.

❖ Roll the napkins and stand them in a ...ide jug or arrange them in a basket.

## TIPS FOR SUCCESSFUL FOLDING

...or folding purposes, heavy linen is ...est, as it becomes firm and crisp when ...tarched. Plain dinner napkins measur-...ng 45–50 cm/18–20 in square, or ...ore, are best and are essential for ...any complicated folding techniques.

❖ The napkins must be cut square and ...he fabric must be cut straight on the ...veave so that the napkins will not pull ...ut of shape easily.

❖ Linen should be washed, starched ...vith traditional starch (spray starch ...vill not give a sufficiently crisp finish) ...nd ironed while damp. When ironing, ...ently pull the napkins back into shape ...f necessary to ensure they are perfectly ...quare again.

❖ It is best to iron napkins on a large ...urface; an ironing board can be too ...arrow when pressing large napkins. ...rotect the surface with a folded thick

towel, which should be covered with a piece of plain white cotton.

❖ Dampen napkins which have dried before ironing. Traditional starch may be mixed and sprayed on linen using a clean plant spray. Allow it to soak into

the fabric for a minute or so before ironing for best results.

When folding napkins into compli-cated shapes, press each fold indi-vidually for best results. Soft folds should not be pressed.

## SIMPLE PRESENTATION

To form a neat square, press the nap-kin, making sure all the corners are perfectly square. Fold it into quarters, pressing each fold. A large quarter-folded napkin may be laid square be-tween the cutlery (flatware) at each place or it may be turned by ninety degrees. This is fine on large tables.

❖ To make a simple triangle, fold the square in half diagonally and press the resulting triangle neatly. Lay the triangular-folded napkin on a side plate, with the long side nearest the place setting. The triangle may also be laid on top of a plate in the middle of the setting.

❖ For a simple oblong, fold a square napkin in half again. This is an ideal way of displaying a decorative corner on the napkin. Plain napkins may be folded and pressed into quarters, then the sides folded underneath and pressed to make an oblong shape. Lay the hemmed edge on the short side at the bottom of the place setting.

❖ Rolled napkins may be kept in place with napkin rings or tied with ribbon or cord. If the napkins are rolled care-fully and laid with the end underneath, they will usually sit quite neatly.

# Pure & Simple

As its name suggests, this design is
quickly arranged and pleasing to the eye.
The outcome is particularly elegant if a
'lace' edged napkin is used.

**1** Start with the corners of the napkin top and
bottom in the form of a diamond. Fold the
corner nearest to you up to meet the top point.
With a finger at the centre bottom, fold the
bottom left point up to the top point.

**2** Fold the right bottom point up to meet the
top point.

**3** Turn the napkin over, keeping the open
corners furthest from you. Fold the bottom
point a third of the way up the napkin.

**4** Carefully tuck both sides under the napkin

# ave

e elegant lines of rippling edges are
own to best effect when folded on a
ue or green napkin.

Fold the top edge of the napkin down to the
ttom. Pick up the top layer at the bottom
ht point and bring the corner over to meet
e bottom left, forming a large triangle.

**2** Carefully turn the napkin over. Lift the top
layer of the bottom right corner and bring it over
to the bottom left, to form a matching triangle
on this side.

**3** Pick up the two right-hand points and bring
them over to the left, slightly splaying all four
points of the napkin.

Roll under a little of the right-hand edge at a
ght angle and pinch to finish.

# Spreading Fan

An elegant yet simple design that is
suitable for all occasions.

**1** Fold up the edge nearest to you to meet the
top edge.

**2** Rotate the napkin so that the folded edge is
on your right. Make equal-sized accordian
pleats all the way up to the top of the napkin,
starting with the edge nearest to you.

**3** Insert the napkin into the ring, or tie with
ribbon or cord and spread out the pleats.

# ndle

s festive fold is the perfect christmas
ch. Green or red napkins are
ticularly suitable.

Starting with the corners of the open napkin
 and bottom in the form of a diamond, fold
e corner nearest to you to meet the top point.
xt fold the bottom edge up a short way to
m a narrow hem.

**2** Hold the hem firmly, and carefully turn over
the napkin so that the long folded edge is to
your right. Then roll up the napkin beginning
from the bottom point and stopping short of the
small top tail.

**3** Turn the candle round so that the tail now
faces you and tuck the tail into the band to
secure the roll.

Tuck the top loose point into the roll and
rm a flame shape with the second loose point
derneath.

## Place Mat

A large, square, cloth napkin can be used as a pretty place mat.

**1** Fold the four corners into the centre.

**2** Place a hand over the middle to hold the corners in position and turn the napkin over.

**3** Fold all four corners of the napkin into the centre again and carefully turn the napkin over for a second time.

**4** Fold each centre corner back to meet the outside corner, and press.

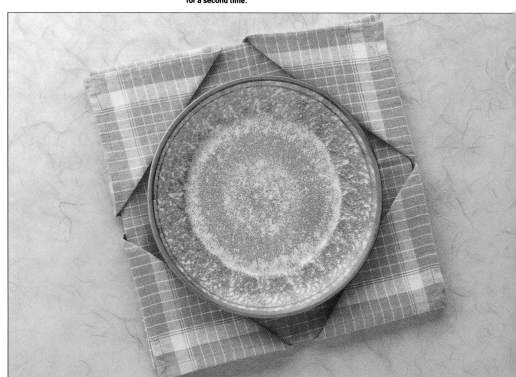

# ffet Parcel

ile balancing a plate in one hand this
fold allows you to carry napkin and
lery at a pinch.

Fold the napkin into quarters. Place a knife
d fork in the centre of the square. Fold in the
side points to form two small triangles.

**2** Bring the two side folds over the cutlery to
cover it completely.

**3** Secure the bundle with ribbon tied in a bow.

# Lover's Knot

This simple design lends a romantic touch to a candle-lit dinner or anniversary breakfast.

**1** Starting with the corners of the open napkin top and bottom in the form of a diamond, fold the top point down to the bottom point.

**2** Starting from the bottom point, make accordion pleats up to the top edge.

**3** With the first pleat facing away from you, fold the right point over the left one and tuck back through the loop created to form a loose but tidy knot.

# ...stival

...dly fanning out, Festival is well suited
...nore colourful napkins and lively
...asions.

...Vith the corners of the open napkin top and
...om in the form of a diamond, fold the
...er nearest to you up to meet the top point.

**2** Make accordion pleats all the way across
the napkin starting from the bottom edge,
gathering each pleat under the last.

**3** Fold the pleated napkin in half from left to
right. Pinch at the fold to hold the shape and
lay out on the plate.

## s in a Glass

s design can create a very striking
splay if folded with a large, colourful
pkin.

*pposite: Iris in a Glass.*

**1** Starting with the corners of the open napkin top and bottom in the form of a diamond, bring the point nearest to you up to the top point to form a triangle.

**2** With a finger at the centre of the fold line, fold up the two corners nearest to you so they are level with the centre top point and slightly to each side of it.

**3** Fold the newly formed bottom point part-way up towards the top point, as shown.

**4** Make accordian pleats across the napkin from left to right. Position the napkin in the glass and fan out the petals of the iris.

## n on a Plate

e a carefully starched linen napkin for
s elegant design.

**1** Fold the napkin in half to form a rectangle. Starting at the edge nearest to you, make eight fairly small, accordian pleats. Press each pleat as you work. Use two-thirds of the rectangle for pleating.

**2** Fold the napkin in half so that the two edges meet on the left and the pleats are on the outside bottom edge.

Fold the top edge – the edge furthest away
m you – down to make a small band. Then
ng top left corner down to the bottom right
d tuck it under the pleats. Turn the napkins
that it stands on the right edge. Then,
lding the bottom with one hand, fan out the
eats.

# Wings

This light-hearted design works best with a stiff cotton napkin and is quick to capture the imagination of young children.

**1** Fold the bottom and top edges of the open napkin into the centre. Bring the bottom fold up to the top.

**2** Fold in the left side by a third.

**3** Fold this side back on itself to align with the outside edge again.

**4** Repeat the process with the right side. Lift the top layers on both sides and curl them back under into their own folds to form the wings.

# ckering Flames

effective yet straightforward design
ich enhances the glassware on your
le. You need two lightweight fringed
th or paper napkins.

Place the two napkins one on top of the
er with all edges aligned. Fold up the edges
arest to you to meet the top edges.

**2** Fold the napkin in half again by bringing the
right edges over to the left edges.

**3** Turn the napkin round, placing the open
corners away from you, and fold the bottom
corner about a third of the way up the napkin.

Make accordion pleats across the napkin
arting from the left point.

Firmly holding the bottom, gently open out
e layers to form the flames and place in glass
finish.

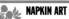

## Candy Cane

For this simple but effective design you
will need two different-coloured cloth or
paper napkins of the same size.

**1** Lay one open napkin on top of the other. Place the top one slightly higher and to the left of the bottom one leaving a small v-shaped border of contrasting colour visible.

**2** Starting with the corner of the V border roll up both napkins together.

**3** Loosely fold the finished roll in half and position.

# anding Christmas Tree

al for the Christmas table, choose a
tive-patterned napkin to make this
nding fold.

Fold the napkin into quarters, keeping the
en corners at the bottom left-hand side. Fold
napkin in half by bringing the top edge
wn towards you.

**2** With a finger at the centre top, lift the
uppermost bottom right corner and bring it over
to meet the bottom left corners.

**3** Carefully turn the napkin over from left to
right. With a hand placed over the left-hand
edge of the napkin, lift the top four bottom
right corners and bring them over to meet the
bottom left point.

Fold the napkin in half down the centre
fore standing it up and straightening into the
r 'branches' of the finished tree.

*Above: Japanese Pleat.*

## Decorative Pocket

This clever design makes an attractive pocket in which to place anything from eating implements to flowers.

**1** Fold the napkin into quarters so that the free edges are facing away from you. Fold the first layer down so that the top corner is just above the bottom corner nearest to you.

*Above: Decorative Poc*

**2** Repeat this process with the second layer, again positioning its top corner just above the one before.

**3** Fold under the side corners until they just overlap at the back.

# panese Pleat

You will need a large starched napkin for this design.

Fold down the edge furthest away from you a third. Fold up the edge nearest to you in e same manner so that the napkin forms a rrow rectangle one-third its original width. ith a finger at the centre top, fold down both des towards you so that the edges meet at e centre.

**2** Holding the diagonal edges, turn the napkin over so that the tip now points towards you and the top layer forms a triangle. Roll down the two extending rectangles towards you until they come just above the base of the triangle.

**3** Grip the rolls firmly with two hands and turn the napkin over again so that the tip of the triangle is facing towards you. Fold the two top corners down so that their edges meet in the centre.

*Below: Gathered Pleat.*

# athered Pleat

sing a simple technique and a napkin ng, create a stylish design for an formal table setting.

Grasp the centre of the napkin and lift it off he table so that the material hangs in soft but early defined folds.

Thread a napkin ring onto the end you are olding and slide it towards the centre. Spread ut the folds to form an attractive shape.

# Table Basket

A cloth napkin can become an attractive basket for breadsticks, crackers or even a dried-flower arrangement.

**1** Fold down the edge furthest away from you by a third. Repeat with the edge nearest to you so that the napkin forms a narrow rectangle one-third its original width. Turn the napkin over so that the free edge is underneath and facing away from you. Fold the right edge to the centre, then fold the left edge to meet the newly formed right edge.

**2** Pull out the first fold made in step 1.

**3** Lift the top edge of the top fold and turn down by one-third, forming a triangle at the

**4** Repeat with the bottom edge of the top fold to form a thin flap. Press.

**5** Fold the narrow flap to your left.

**6** Now fold the wide right edge to meet the narrow left edge.

Follow steps 3 and 4 on the second side.

**8** Fold the narrow flap on the second side to your right.

**9** Holding the flaps at the centre, turn the napkin inside out. (The flaps form the lining of the rectangular basket.)

## oll-top

is is an easy napkin fold that will grace oth an informal and formal table setting. e 'pockets' are ideal for presenting me cards, or perhaps a small gift on ecial occasions.

**1** Fold down the edge furthest away from you by a third. Then fold up the edge nearest to you in the same manner so that the napkin forms a narrow rectangle one-third its original width.

**2** Fold the left and right edges over by about 5cm/2in towards the centre – adjust the size of this band according to the size of the napkin.

To form the first 'pocket', bring the right side the napkin across to the left, leaving the t-hand band uncovered but its raw edge ncealed.

Fold from the right side again, making sure at each 'pocket' measures the same width.

# Valentine Heart

For this romantic shape you need a napkin
that will hold a crease.

**1** Fold the napkin in half bringing the top edge
down towards you.

**2** Fold it almost in half again bringing the
bottom edges up just short of the top.

**3** With a finger at the centre bottom, fold the
sides up to meet in the middle.

**4** Turn the napkin over, keeping the point
towards you. Fold in each of the four top
corners so that you make four small triangles.
Reverse to finish.

# ouble Fan

is classic design is ideal for more
rmal dinners but it requires a little time
practise it. You will need a large,
arched cotton napkin.

Fold the bottom and top edges of the napkin
meet in the centre and fold in half by
nging the bottom edge up to the top.

**2** Turn the napkin so that a short edge faces
you and fold it seven times to make eight
accordion pleats.

**3** Grasp the bottom of the pleats firmly and in
between each pleat pull the layer nearest to
you down to form double-layered triangles.

Turn the napkin round and repeat the
ocess on the other side. Spread the folds out
to the fan shape.

# G.I. Cap

This children's favourite may make it difficult to stop hats being worn at the table! It works well in khaki, green or grey.

**1** Bring down the edge furthest from you to fold the napkin in half. Fold the left edge into the centre.

**2** Do the same with the right edge. Holding the top layer of the folded-in right edge half-way up, lift it out to the right again while holding the bottom layer in place also from half-way up. Flatten to make a triangular shape at the top.

**3** Do the same with the top layer of the folde in left side and open out in the same way. Fo both sides underneath.

**4** Fold the uppermost bottom flap up to mee the bottom edge of the triangles.

**5** Fold the flap again so that it half covers th triangles. Turn the napkin over and repeat th final two folds on the other flap. Hollow out a put a dent in the top crease to make the finished cap.

# boat

jolly arrangement can easily be
mented with sea-related pieces, such
hells or pebbles.

old the open napkin into quarters. Keep the
n corners nearest to you and fold them up
he top point.

**2** With a finger placed at the top point, fold
down the right and left sides by bringing each
point towards you.

**3** Next turn the napkin over and fold up the
bottom point.

Turn the napkin over again and fold it in half
ckwards along the centre line. Hold the
tom firmly and open out the top layers to
ke the sails of the boat.

# Cable Buffet

This smart design allows guests at a
buffet or picnic to help themselves to
napkin and cutlery all at once.

**1** Fold the bottom edge of the napkin up to the
top. Next fold the top layer down to meet the
bottom edge.

**2** Fold all the bottom layers back up a little
way and turn the napkin over. To make a longer
design you can turn up only the upper bottom
layer as in the main picture.

**3** Bring the right side into the centre.

**4** Bring the left side into the centre.

**5** Tuck one half of the napkin deep into the
other half locking the napkin flat. Turn over to
insert cutlery into the pocket.

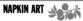

# Crown

rown is one of the better-known
tional napkin folds and is often seen
staurants. It can be used to cover a
ned bread roll at each place setting,
uld hide a surprise for each guest.

ld the edge nearest to you to meet the top
.

**2** Fold the bottom right corner of the napkin up to the middle right.

**3** Fold the top left corner down.

urn the napkin over. Make sure that the
folded edges are directly facing you top
bottom. Fold over the top edge – the edge
hest away from you – to meet the edge
rest to you.

**5** Release the second point which is still tucked under so that there are two triangles at the top.

**6** Tuck the bottom left point under the edge of the right triangle. Carefully turn the napkin over and repeat the step.

Gently open out at the bottom to form a
le and stand the crown up.

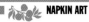 

## Papillon

The brighter and more varied the patterned napkin used, the more effective your butterfly will emerge. Begin with the patterned side up.

**1** Fold the bottom edge of the open napkin up to the top. Fold the top left and top right corners down to meet at the bottom edge.

**2** Turn the napkin over and fold in the left-hand side to make a point facing you.

**3** Fold in the right-hand side in the same w Allow the two loose layers from underneath napkin to open out on each side.

**4** Turn the napkin over so that the two loos points are facing you. Fold down the top po to tuck it into the pocket formed by the horizontal edge.

**5** Placing a hand on each side of the centre push together a small section from each si create the butterfly's body. The upper wing should move slightly upwards while the tail wing tips should move apart.

# rasol

ain or patterned napkin would be
ropriate for this attractive design.
'll also need a short length of
trasting ribbon for the finishing touch.

Make accordion pleats with the whole open
kin, beginning at the edge nearest to you.

**2** Place one hand firmly over the centre of the
completed pleats and bring the left edges over
to the right edges, folding the napkin in half.

**3** Tie a bow half-way up the pleats and then
fan out the top to make the parasol.

# Fanned Bow

The fanned bow is perfect for festive
occasions, especially if you use a highly
decorative napkin ring or shiny ribbon tied
into a bow.

**1** Fold the top and bottom edges of the napkin
to meet in the middle to form a rectangle.

**2** Rotate the napkin so that the shorter edges
are facing you top and bottom. Starting at the
edge nearest to you, accordian-pleat the
napkin, pressing each pleat as you work.

**3** Thread a wide napkin ring along to the
centre of the napkin, or tie with ribbon. Fa
the pleats to make a circular bow.

# ...ned Pleats

...s is a quick and easy design for the ...inner.

...Fold the bottom left corner of the napkin to ... top right corner.

**2** Fold the resulting triangle in half, bringing the bottom right corner up to the highest point, with the top point of the napkin slightly to the left of the bottom point.

**3** Fold the triangle in half again to create three points, bringing the top point up and to the right of the other two points.

...old the top left corner under the napkin to ... it a slender, elegant shape.

# Pinwheel

An amusing party piece which will
especially appeal to children

**1** Fold the four corners into the centre.

**2** Fold the top edge and the bottom edge into
the centre.

**3** Bring the left and right sides into the cent

**4** Gently find each of the four loose corners
the centre and bring them out to the side to
form four points.

**5** Fold the bottom left point to the left-hand
side and the top right point to the right.

# ck Step

duck step is a basic napkin fold that is
metrically pleasing and easy to
struct.

Fold the bottom edge of the open napkin up
he top. Fold the napkin in half again.

**2** Fold down the left side.

**3** Fold down the right side to meet it in the
centre. Carefully turn the napkin over.

Keeping hold of the centre line, fold the two
es back.

Separate the two square flaps and lay them
t so that the pointed centre fold stands up.

# Shirt

This is a clever design which is much easier to make up than it looks!

**1** Fold the four corners into the centre.

**2** Next fold the top edge and the bottom edge into the centre.

**3** Turn the right edge underneath to form a small hem.

**4** Fold the bottom right and top right corners into the centre line to meet about the margin's width from the right edge.

**5** With a hand firmly keeping the completed folds in place and a thumb at the centre of the napkin, fold out the two corners on the left.

**6** Gently lift up the left edge and fold it over to the right, carefully tucking it under the points of the 'collar'.

# Double Jabot

This elegant geometric design suits a smarter occasion or formal sitting.

**1** Fold the napkin into quarters, keeping the open corners facing away from you. Accordion-pleat the top layer from the top point down to just below the centre line.

**2** Repeat the process with the next layer finishing on the other side of the centre line.

**3** Firmly holding the pleats in place, fold the right half of the napkin under the left half to form a triangle.

**4** Bring the two points from the long edge together, tucking one inside the other to secure the napkin. Stand the napkin with the pleats facing outwards.

# ometric Style

-catching and elegant, this is a
dern design suitable for an up-beat
asion.

Starting with the corners of the open napkin
and bottom in the form of a diamond, fold
top corner down to the bottom corner. With
ger at the bottom point, fold the left side in
eet the centre line.

**2** Fold the right side into the centre. Fold the
left point into the centre again.

**3** Fold the right point into the centre.

Turn the napkin over, still keeping the long
nt facing you. Bring the bottom point up to
et the top, folding the napkin in half.

Tuck the long point into the horizontal fold
d reverse.

# Elf's Boot

For this entertaining design use a cloth or large paper napkin. Be sure to place the finished boot the right way up to catch the diner's attention.

**1** Fold the top and bottom edges of the napkin to meet in the middle to form a rectangle. Bring the bottom edge to meet the top edge, folding the rectangle in half.

**2** With a finger at the centre bottom, fold up both sides away from you so that the edges meet in the middle.

**3** Fold the right and left sides closest to you into the centre to form a sharper point.

**4** Fold the left side over onto the right side.

**5** Move the napkin round so the bottom point now faces to your right. Fold the top left tail down towards you.

**6** Fold the bottom edge of the other left tail upwards and tuck the tail securely into the pocket of the tail on the right.

## Picnic Pocket

This practical idea keeps the cutlery tidy and, as it uses two napkins, provides a tablemat as well as a napkin when opened. You will need two napkins of different colours.

**1** Place the two napkins one on top of the other with the top one slightly lower down and overlapping a little. Fold both napkins in half from left to right.

**2** Lay the cutlery along the centre of the napkins and fold the side edges over to enclose it.

**3** Fold the bottom edge up by about a third.

**4** Bring down the top edge and tuck it into the folded bottom edge.

# op's Hat

s a very traditional method of folding
dinner napkins. The proportions are
rtant, so it may be necessary to
st some of the folds as you work it
igh.

tarting with the corners of the open napkin
and bottom in the form of a diamond, fold
corner nearest to you to just below the
er furthest away from you to form a
gle.

**2** Fold up the two corners nearest to you until
the edges align.

**3** Bring the newly created bottom corner up
and away from you so that its top edge sits just
below the first corner when folded.

old down the front edge.

3end the left and right corners backwards
I interlock one half into the other to form a
e that will not spring open.

# Corsage

To make this attractive design it is best to use a small napkin centred inside another one approximately one third larger. The two can then be folded together as one.

**1** One by one, lift up all four points of the larger napkin and bring them neatly together.

**2** Tightly holding the points together, pull the napkin along the looped edges until it flattens into a square shape when placed on its side.

**3** With the open corners facing away from you, fold the right and left bottom edges of the top layer into the centre. Carefully turn the napkin over and repeat the process with the edges on this side.

**4** Fold the bottom point up to meet the horizontal edges.

**5** Fold the bottom half of the napkin together.

**6** Holding the bottom firmly in one hand, gently spread out the open top layers.

## Pure Elegance

Easy to construct, this design is ideal for
both formal dining and a low-key setting.

**1** Fold the bottom edge up by a third and fold
the top third of the napkin down over it.

**2** Turn the napkin so that a short edge is
nearest to you. Fold the top edge down to the
centre and repeat with the bottom edge.

**3** Fold the top left corner and bottom left
corner into the centre and turn the napkin
so that the pointed edge faces towards you

**4** Bring both top points down towards eac
other and tuck the right point inside the po
underneath the left point. To position, turn
napkin around and stand.

# n's Hat

erfect start to a birthday feast, this
gement is seen at its best in bold or
d colours.

ld the top edge of the open napkin down
eet the bottom edge. Next bring the top
corner down to the centre bottom.

**2** Fold the bottom right point over to the
bottom left corner.

**3** Next bring the bottom right corner up to
meet the top left point, folding the napkin in
half diagonally.

vide the eight layers on the left into two
ps of four. Fold both groups back to form a
l hem. Hollow out the napkin to form a
shape.

uck the small tail into the rim of the hat to
plete the fold.

# Spring Time

For this slightly more complicated design a large cloth or paper napkin that will hold a crease is needed. Place the patterned or 'good' side of the napkin face down.

**1** Fold the napkin in half with the fold at the top. Lift the bottom of the top layer and make accordion pleats up to the edge furthest away from you.

**2** Grasp the pleats firmly and turn the napkin over so that the pleats are underneath and nearest to you. With a thumb at the centre bottom, fold up the two sides so that the pleats meet in the centre.

**3** Gently turn the napkin over again from t bottom. Fold the bottom right and left corne tucking them into the pocket at the top poi

**4** Next bring down the top point, folding the napkin in half.

**5** Fold this point up again away from you but only enough so that it extends slightly beyond the top edge.

**6** Lift each side corner in towards each oth and tuck one inside the other.

**7** Carefully turn the napkin over and fan out the pleats to finish the butterfly.

## Diagonal Pockets

A smart design suitable for any occasion.
Use the pockets for decorative
accessories, such as a small flower, a
sprig of herbs or perhaps a small gift.

**1** Fold the napkin into quarters, making sure
that all the open corners are at the top right-
hand side. Roll the top layer back diagonally
towards you as far as it will go.

**2** Press the roll flat to form a thin band.

**3** Bring the second layer back and tuck the
corner behind the first band until the folded
edge forms a parallel band the same width
the first.

**4** Repeat the process with the third layer.

**5** Fold the sides under to the back to form a
neat rectangle.

# er Lily

design requires a well-starched
in to make the cup shape. It can be
to hold a bread roll, a small gift or
onal decorations such as small fir
s and holly at Christmas, chocolate
ts for Valentine's Day, or a tiny posy
ring flowers.

**1** Fold the corners of the napkin into the
centre and press flat.

**2** Repeat the process a second time.

olding the centre points together, carefully
the napkin over.

**4** Fold the four corners into the centre again,
but do not press.

**5** Holding the centre firmly, partly pull out the
previous fold from under each corner and
gently pull them upward to make the petals.

ull out the corners from underneath
veen the petals, to form the base leaves of
lily.

# Bunny Rabbit

These cheeky bunny ears are the perfect table greeting for young party goers. The brighter the napkin used, the better!

**1** Fold the top and bottom edges of the open napkin to meet in the centre.

**2** Fold in half by bringing the bottom side up to the top edge.

**3** With a finger at the centre bottom, fold both sides away from you so that the edges meet in the centre.

**4** Fold the left and right top corners down into the centre.

**5** Next fold each top outside edge into the centre making two narrow points facing away from you.

**6** Holding the napkin in your left hand fold bottom point underneath.

**7** Bring the two bottom points this forms towards each other and interlock one point into the triangular pocket of the other.

**8** Using a finger inside the base of the napkin, gently shape it to make it round.

**9** Carefully turn the napkin over and open out the bottom folds to make the face.

# STUNNING SETTINGS

*they pass through the hallway before dinner, the merest glimpse of arrangements should excite the dining instincts, hinting at the quality of the meal to come.*

*Whether crisp and sophisticated, softly flowing with lc and flowers, warm and homely, or refreshingly bright, th setting should confirm the guests' anticipation of the party and raise it to new levels. This section is designed to arou your enthusiasm for scene-setting and to encourage artisti instincts. With flair and a sense of occasion you can be as individualistic as you wish, and carry off any event with outstanding success.*

*T*he first sight of the table plays a keynote for any meal, so it is essential that the setting is just right for the occasion. In contemporary living-dining rooms and at buffet parties the table is on display from the moment the guests arrive; if guests happen to pass an open dining room door as

## TABLE LINEN

There is an enormous variety of table linen available, most of it far removed from traditional white linen. There are no rules about what is acceptable or otherwise, the only qualification being that the choice should suit the occasion. A chequered patio cloth and bright paper napkins are not worthy of a gourmet meal of classic dishes. Conversely white damask and fine glass would seem inappropriate for a casual invitation for a snack lunch . . . .

## White linen

White linen is both versatile and practical, and there is nothing quite like crisply starched, large white napkins for a dinner party table.

Heavy, white damask tablecloths and napkins are expensive but they will last for years. It is always worth looking out for good-quality second-hand linen at auctions, flea markets and in antique or junk shops – as long as the fabric is not scorched, badly marked, worn or torn, then it is a good buy.

Although spray starch is adequate for a tablecloth, the only way to get a really good finish on napkins is by starching them with traditional starch which you mix with boiling water. A good compromise, instead of soaking

the fabric in the starch solution, is to mix a small quantity according to the packet directions, then keep it in a clean plant spray bottle. Spray dry napkins and cloths before ironing, leaving the moisture to soak into the fabric for about 30 seconds. The result

is just like proper starched linen.

Although plain white linen is ur able for casual table settings, do feel that it always has to form the for extremely formal table arr ments. Introduce a contemporar with your choice of flowers or

*White, damask table linen adds elegance to a formal dinner.*

*...ose brightly coloured table linen for an ethnic meal or theme party.*

...trepieces; instead of traditional ...ite candles go for coloured ones or ...n scented candles; or neatly roll the ...kins and use colourful napkin ties ...ribbons with a small flower or suit- ...e trimming to pick up on the rest of ... table decorations.

**...in and Printed Linen**

...od linen in delicate pastel shades can ...equally as formal as traditional ...ite table settings. Deep colours can ...more dramatic and stylish but just as ...mal, depending on the overall pre- ...tation. Strong colours can also

make an eye-catching base for flamboyant themes, particularly when preparing an ethnic meal or for fancy dress

### Table Protection
Buy a waterproof protective covering to lay on the table under the cloth. This protects the table surface from plates and glassware, and from any spills. Do not buy a cheap brand if you have a good table; it is better to spend more and know that the table is safe.

(costume) parties and buffets.

Printed and woven linen varies enormously in quality. Smart checks and stripes are useful for informal picnics, barbecues, patio meals, breakfasts and brunches.

**Embroidered Linen and Lace**

Colourful hand embroidery is ideal for breakfast cloths, and for table coverings for brunches, family teas and high tea. Fine work trimmed with lace and lace cloths are ideal for afternoon teas, parties in the garden, grand picnic parties and for weddings.

*A garland of fresh flowers and foliage enhances an outdoor buffet table.*

## BUFFET SETTINGS

Buffet tables provide the perfect excuse for impressive settings, perhaps with swags of flowers or ribbons and posies as well as a large main decoration. All the food should be decorative too, and it must be arranged for ease of access when guests serve themselves.

The buffet may be placed against a wall so that guests move along in front of the table and serve themselves, or it may be situated in the middle of a room (or with space all around) so that guests move around the table. Whichever system is used, there should be an obvious starting point for serving and this is indicated by a pile of plates. On a large table, plates may be piled at both ends so that guests can work from both directions.

If the buffet is set against a wall, then the main decoration should be at the

*Small garlands look pretty above entrances.*

rear and positioned in the centre. If guests walk all around the table, then a centrepiece should be placed on the table.

Make sure all the dishes are easy to reach and that there are serving spoons nearby. If there is a ham or other food

which needs carving, set it in a posit to one side of the table so that guests not obstruct access to other dis while they carve. It should be sor one's task to check the availability foods, topping dishes up and tidy the buffet occasionally.

Set napkins and cutlery separately a side table. Large paper napkins usually used for informal buffets. disposable plates are used, they sho be sturdy and of good quality, as t plates sag miserably and make eat difficult. Buffet-style plates are n available which include a holder fc wine glass. Alternatively, keep a la number of good-quality, large pla plates, which are ideal for entertain in large numbers. They are easier rinse, stack and wash than china pla and ideal for outdoor parties as wel for informal buffets.

### Themed Settings

There are times when it is fun to abandon convention and go for something strikingly different in the way of setting arrangements. This is fine if you know the guests reasonably well, but it is not a good idea to confront business acquaintances or people you only meet with something out of the ordinary. Think of these setting styles as informal alternatives!

White and pastels tend to be favoured colours for table settings, but strong colours make a dramatic impact. A blue and gold setting, for example, could have a deep blue cloth and napkins, matching candles and a blue flower arrangement, such as hydrangeas, hyacinths, delphiniums, lavender or cornflowers. Wire dried autumn leaves and spray them gold, then use these with the fresh flowers.

Alternatively, try creating a lush green table using a white linen cloth as the base and limiting the other colour to green, including candles. Make a central arrangement of leaves: as well as cuttings from shrubs, take leaves from indoor plants, such as Japanese aralia and grape ivy. Create movement and interest by using leaves of different sizes and shapes.

A contrast setting could start with a black tablecloth and white dinner plates. Use black-and-white napkins, perhaps ones that have a strong, geometric pattern. To make an elongated napkin shape with points at the top and bottom, fold and press each

Combine clean lines and black and white chinaware and table linen for a strikingly modern look.

napkin into quarters, then give it a quarter turn and fold the opposite side corners over the middle so that they overlap. Press neatly and place one on each plate.

Use small white candle holders and short black candles, or small white saucers and black nightlights (votive-style candles) or small, rounded candles. Place several of these along the length of a rectangular table or around the middle of a circular table. If using white saucers, press and fold two small squares of crêpe paper to sit under the candles: one black square to go on the saucer, then a white square offset on top to go under the candle.

Any central decoration should be simple and based on white flowers with dried leaves that are wired and sprayed black.

In complete contrast, a pretty lace setting is ideal for a celebratory lu party, for a small wedding lunch p or for a large buffet table. Lay a pl coloured cloth or fabric over the tal pink is ideal for this theme. The co should be reasonably strong but garish. Lay a lace cloth over the p cloth so that the colour shows throu

*Opposite: fine lace and small posies of flowe set the scene for a celebration lunch.*

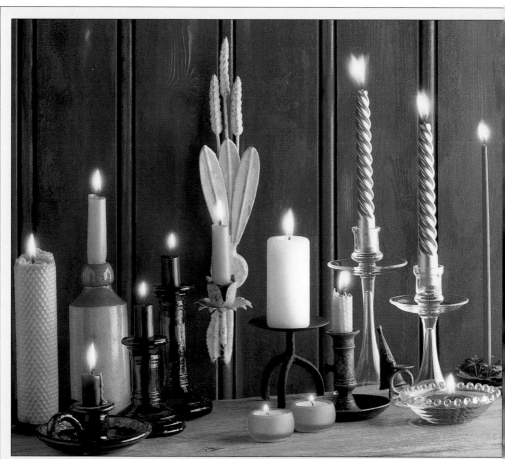

*Candles and candle holders come in a wide range of sizes and colours suitable for every occasion.*

## Lighting for Effect

Fixing on the right lighting is crucial to the success of any scene-setting plan and the results can have marked effects on your guests. Just as people will feel uncomfortable in glaringly bright surroundings more conducive to a dentist's office than to a dinner party, so they will also feel unnerved and depressed by lighting which is dim to the point of being gloomy.

For the majority of entertaining the lighting should be soft enough to make your guests look their best and to suggest that everyone ought to be relaxed. It should, however, be bright enough for people to see what is being eaten and to read the expressions across the dining table.

## Candles

Candles really do give a room a pleasing glow. They should be used in conjunction with sufficient electric light to ensure that the surroundings are bright enough.

❖ Slim, tall candles are perfect for elegant dining.

❖ Chubby, bright candles are well suited to kitchen suppers and informal meals.

❖ Create different heights of light by arranging candles around the room. Place some on a fireplace hearth (set them to one side if the fire is lit, otherwise they melt and run), others on side tables and some at windowsill level.

❖ Arrange marbles or glass pebbles in a large copper or other metal bowl with nightlights. Place the bowl on a low table or footstool in a corner of the room.

❖ Wherever you place candles, make absolutely sure that they present no risk of fire and never leave lit candles unattended.

❖ Floating candles are designed for floating when alight. Select a wide-topped glass bowl and place some colourful stones, shells and artificial aquarium plants in the bowl. Float and light the candles.

❖ Combine floating candles and Japanese water flowers.

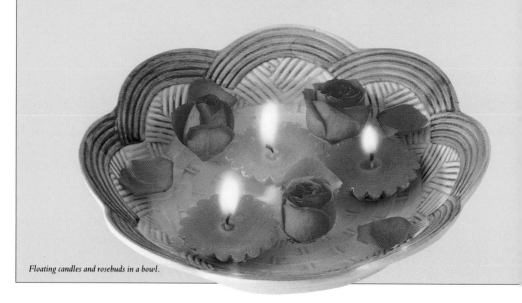

*Floating candles and rosebuds in a bowl.*

Set conventional place settings. Roll the napkins and tie them with satin ribbon and large bows.

Draw up the lace cloth at the corners of the table and at intervals around the edge (between place settings), then pin it in place so that it hangs in swags.

Prepare small posies of roses and tie them with flamboyant bows of satin ribbon to match the place settings. Pin the flowers on the cloth.

Arrange a large bowl of roses for the centre of the table. Make sure you have enough roses to lay one at each place

setting. Trim each stem and wrap v a leaf in a little moistened absorb kitchen paper (paper towels). A f wrapping of foil will hold everyth together and keep in the moist Place the roses under the bows arot the napkins shortly before guests arr

### Candles
White candles are traditional at for dinners but this convention depe entirely on the hostess and the setti Tall candlesticks usually have sl candles and short holders take l candles. The candles may be place the centre of the table or at inter along its length. If there is the sp very effective settings can be create flouting this convention and arrang low candles or nightlights (votive-s candles) towards the table corners.

### Ideas for Electric Lights

❖ Arrange fans or sunshades in front of floor spotlights to create a warm light.

❖ Make large paper lanterns and place very low-wattage bulbs in them (15 watt).

❖ Use coloured bulbs. These are especially good for lively parties,

where areas may be lit with bright red, blue or green by fitting the appropriate bulbs.

❖ Use a floor spotlight or standard spotlight to cast light from behind a large, exotic-looking indoor plant – the effect can be quite eerie.

❖ Place a low-wattage light on a windowsill to illuminate a hand-painted blind or unusual fabric.

# bbon Rosette

is simply made old-fashioned idea is a
assic trim for swathes of filmy fabric.

**OU WILL NEED:** firm satin ribbon about
.5 cm/1 in wide in two toning shades:
oout 1.8 m/2 yd in deeper tone and
out 90 cm/1 yd in paler tone, scissors,
edle and thread.

**1** Cut seven 17.5 cm/7 in lengths of deeper-
toned ribbon and tie a single knot fairly loosely
in the middle of each.

**2** Twist the ends of one of the knotted pieces
of ribbon so that they lie on top of one another.

Twist a second piece of ribbon in the same
y and hold the ends together, with the knots
g side by side.

**4** Continue to arrange all seven pieces of
ribbon into an overlapping circle, knots evenly
spaced around the edge and ends gathered in
the centre. Secure the ends with a few
stitches.

**5** Cut five 17.5 cm/7 in lengths of paler-toned
ribbon and tie in knots as before. Arrange them
in the centre of the rosette and stitch in place.

Make a small loop of darker ribbon. Sew this
he centre of the rosette to conceal the ends
d stitching, puckering it gently to make an
ractive shape. Sew two long tail pieces of
oon to the back of the rosette.

## Appliqué Napkin

Appliqué in the form of flowers or fruit makes decorative corner trimmings for plain tablecloths and napkins.

**YOU WILL NEED:** plain coloured napkins, thin card (posterboard) for template, pencil, colourfast red fabric, green felt, scissors, iron-on interfacing, dressmaker's marking pen, red and yellow thread, needle.

**1** Transfer the strawberry shape to the red fabric and the stem shape to the green felt. You will also need to transfer the strawberry shape onto a piece of iron-on interfacing.

**2** Cut around the lines using a pair of sharp scissors. Iron on the interfacing to the back of the strawberry cut-out. Mark where the seed details will go with a dressmaker's marking pen (this should be washable).

**3** Tack (baste) the strawberry cut-out in pla on the napkin, then stitch all around the ed using buttonhole stitch or zig-zag machine stitch. This will prevent the fabric from fray Tack the stem in position, then hand or machine stitch in place using a straight sti and yellow thread. Hand stitch the seed de using the yellow thread.

## ncilled Table Linen

stencils used as part of the dining or kitchen decor can be picked up on ns and napkins using fabric paints. Do ry to match colours, as it is unlikely will be able to achieve the same

shade with fabric paints. Select toning or contrasting colours instead. Follow the manufacturer's instructions for using fabric paint for a result which is lasting and washable.

**YOU WILL NEED:** plain coloured place mats and napkins; (for making stencil) paper, pencil, sticky (transparent) tape; clear acetate for stencil, waterproof black felt-tip pen, craft knife, fabric paints, paintbrush, rag.

you are making your own stencil, draw design onto a sheet of paper. Place the et of acetate on top and tape in position to the sheet firmly in place. Transfer the gn to the acetate using a waterproof black tip pen. Cut around the outline of the cil design with a craft knife.

oad the brush with paint. Keep a rag handy viping excess paint from the brush. For ncilling, you should not have too much paint he brush as this can seep beneath the cil. Holding the stencil firmly in place, s the brush over the pattern in the stencil ping the brush vertical. Wait for the paint to before applying the second colour.

o create a stippled effect, you will need ne white or pale coloured paint and a clean sh. Lightly load the brush with paint and dab he paint using a stabbing motion. Allow the nt to dry, then fix according to the nufacturer's instructions.

## Gold Leaf Napkin Ring

Collect autumn leaves to make this elegant napkin ring. Dried beech leaves have been used here, but any medium-sized dried leaves are suitable. As an alternative, use silver spray to paint.

**YOU WILL NEED:** dried leaves, wire, gold spray paint, florists' dry foam (styro foam), heavy satin ribbon, needle and matching thread.

**1** For each napkin ring, wire 3 dried leaves onto 20 cm/8 in wires.

**2** Spray the wired leaves with gold spray paint on a well-protected work surface. Always work in a well-ventilated area. Stand each finished leaf in florists' dry foam (styro foam) to dry.

**3** When the paint is dry, twist the leaves together. Arrange the leaves so that the ce leaf is higher than the other two leaves. All about 2.5 cm/1 in of wire to remain untwist immediately below the leaves when they h been arranged.

**4** Wrap the end of the ribbon around the wire below the middle leaf, taking about 7.5 cm/3 in of the end and binding it around the twisted wire. Bind another layer of ribbon over this, then bind along the length of the wire.

**5** Stitch the ribbon in place at the end of the wire with matching thread. Trim off any protuding ends of wire. Form the ribboned wire into a ring and secure the end under the leaves with a few stitches. Gently twist the leaves in place and flatten the ring to neaten.

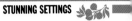

## eenery Chain

ke a simple chain of greenery to swag
 table edge.

**J WILL NEED:** suitable foliage, plastic-
ered tying wire or florists' wire,
ection of herbs such as bay leaves,
emary and thyme, needle and green
ead, pins, green ribbon.

**1**  Join lengths of foliage together with suitable
wire cut into manageable strips.

**2**  Wire sprigs of herbs and stitch them to the
chain at intervals. Pin the chain to one corner
of the table and then pin at each sprig of herbs
to form swags. Trim with bows of green ribbon.

# Standing Place Cards

Place cards are always laid at formal or large dinners. Simple, elegant cards are best for such occasions. Lay them in a suitable position on the setting, such as on a side plate or with the napkin.

**YOU WILL NEED:** card (posterboard); (for making stencil) paper, pencil, sticky (transparent) tape; craft knife, stencil or sheet of acetate, waterproof black felt-tip pen, gold paint, stencil brush, thin coloured ribbon.

**1** Cut a strip of card (posterboard) measuring 15 × 7.5 cm/6 × 3 in. Mark a fold across the centre of the card and a 2.5 cm/1 in fold at each end of the strip. Lightly score the folds with a craft knife, but be careful not to cut through the card.

**2** If you are making your own stencil, draw your design onto a sheet of paper. Place the sheet of acetate on top and tape in position to hold the sheet firmly in place. Transfer the design to the acetate using a waterproof black felt-tip pen. Cut around the outline of the design using the craft knife. Lightly load the brush with gold paint. Holding the stencil firmly in position, press the brush over the pattern in the stencil keeping the brush vertical.

**3** To attach the ribbon, mark and then cut small slits in the card. Thread the ribbon through and tie into a bow. Trim the ends of ribbon if necessary.

# t-out Place Cards

patterned card (posterboard) for
se attractive place cards: special
bled, coloured, gold or silver card is
able.

**YOU WILL NEED:** plain card, patterned
card, tracing paper, pencil, craft knife,
glue.

or each place card, you will need a strip of
terned card (posterboard) measuring 20 ×
cm/8 × 4 in. Trace the pattern for the
out area onto tracing paper. Using a soft
cil, shade the area underneath the tracing.
k a fold across the centre of the card and a
cm/1 in fold at each end of the strip. Lightly
re the folds with a craft knife, but do not cut
ugh the card. Lay the tracing shaded side
n on the reverse of one half of the
erned card, positioned centrally. Using a
rp pencil, follow the line of the design.

**2** On a hard surface, use the craft knife to cut
out the shape.

**3** Push the cut-out area from the right side of
the card, *not* from the back. Take care to push
out any intricate designs carefully.

ut out a strip of plain card measuring 9.5 ×
/3¾ × 2¾ in. Stick the plain card behind
cut-out area on the patterned card with
.

# Flower Rope

A single flower rope adds decoration to an awkward panel of wall — beside a door for example. A pair looks elegant framing a fireplace. Alternatively, a series of ropes

can be suspended at links in paper chains or swags of ribbon. Hung from table edges, they create a very festive atmosphere.

**YOU WILL NEED:** green raffia, florists' wire, florists' tape, pins, flower heads such as orchids, lilies etc, foliage suc ivy, ruscus etc, narrow and wide matcl ribbon.

**1** Tie a knot at one end of the bundle of raffia, divide the strands into three and plait (braid) loosely. Trim the end to length and secure.

**2** Make a loop at one end of a length of florists' wire and wire individual ivy leaves.

**3** Hold an ivy leaf and an orchid together twist the wire around both stems. Bind bot stems together with florists' tape.

**4** Wire and tape together other flower heads and leaves. Insert an orchid and ivy leaf near the top of the raffia rope.

**5** Insert a second wired flower head into the raffia rope below the orchid, positioning it at an attractive angle to add width.

**6** Continue to add further flower heads an leaves, alternating the angles to achieve a balanced effect. Position one flower head conceal the end of the raffia rope.

**7** Wind a trail of ruscus leaves around the raffia rope, tucking it in behind the flowers Make little long-tailed bows with narrow ribbon, and curl the ends.

**8** Attach the little bows to the raffia with p Arrange a spray of ivy to add width at the t the rope and wire in place. Attach a large ribbon bow at the top.

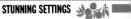

# iky Paper Flowers

paper of a single colour for each
om, or make each layer from a
erent shade – for example, from pink
ough mauve and violet to blue – for a
wing, luminous effect. Crêpe paper
kes suitably chunky leaves to contrast
h the delicate flowers.

**YOU WILL NEED:** 20 cm/8 in squares of
tissue paper in flower colours and crêpe
paper in green, florists' wire, small paper
scissors, needle.

end a small loop in one end of a length of
. Fold four sheets of tissue paper together
quarters. Beginning about 2.5 cm/1 in
y from the central corner, cut a circle of
es radiating out towards the outer edges of
paper.

**2** Open out the folds and use a needle to make
a hole through the centre. Push the straight
end of the wire through the hole. Separate the
tissue paper layers and rotate them slightly to
stagger them.

**3** Turn the flower over and gently gather the
petals over the wire loop. Holding the bottom of
the flower between thumb and forefinger, twist
the wire two or three times around the centre of
the paper to secure.

Fold the sheets of crêpe paper in half and
out leaf shapes. Wire these in the same
y and arrange between and around the
wers.

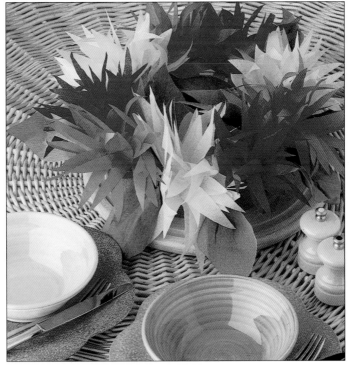

# Felt Flower Napkin Rings

Choose fine, smooth felt and ribbon in colours to match or harmonize with your table settings.

**YOU WILL NEED:** (for each napkin ring) thin card (posterboard) for template, pencil, scissors, coloured and green felt, needle and thread to match, a few tiny beads; (for each felt flower) 90 cm/1 yd velvet ribbon about 1.5 cm/⅝ in wide, needle and thread to match, 20 cm/8 in plastic-covered tying wire, wire cutters.

**1** Cut out two circular templates, one 6.5 cm/ 2½ in in diameter and the other 4 cm/1½ in. Draw the outlines onto the felt and cut out.

**2** Fold each felt circle in quarters and cut a shallow V-shape out of the curved edge to make scalloped 'petals'.

**3** Sew a tiny ring of running stitches aroun the centre of each flower shape, then pull t thread to pucker the centre slightly.

**4** Stitch the smaller circle on top of the larger one. Sew three or four beads in the centre.

**5** Cut out two leaf shapes from green felt.

**6** Place the leaves on the underside of the flower and stitch.

**7** Cut the ribbon into three equal lengths. Stitch the ribbon lengths together at one end with matching thread.

**8** Plait (braid) the ribbon neatly and not too tightly so that it forms an even band.

**9** Secure the end of the plait with a few stitches and trim.

**10** Run a length of plastic-covered tying wire along the back of the plait, securing it in place with a few stitches here and there.

**11** Form the plait into a ring, twisting the ends of the wire together to secure. Trim off the excess wire with wire cutters. Turn the ends of the plait under and stitch together.

**12** Sew the flower to the plait to cover the join.

*continued . . .*    73

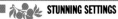 

*continued .*

A red poppy napkin ring will bring a splash of colour to a summer lunch table. The plaited (braided) ring is made in the same way as before.

**YOU WILL NEED:** (for each poppy) thin card (posterboard) for template, pencil, scissors, red felt, needle and thread to match, black haberdashers' wire for stamens; (for each napkin ring) 90 cm/1 yd velvet ribbon, 20 cm/8 in plastic-covered tying wire, wire cutters.

**13** Make a card template for a three-lobed poppy shape about 7.5 cm/3 in in diameter. Draw the outline onto the felt.

**14** Cut out two poppy shapes for each flower.

**15** Fold the flower to find the centre and cut tiny nick with scissors.

**16** Lay the two poppy shapes together with the lobes at different angles. Shape hooked stamens using haberdashers' wire.

**17** Insert the stamens into the centre of the poppy from front to back. Twist the wire around the base of the flower once or twice.

**18** Stitch the wire to the base of the poppy to secure. Attach the poppy to the plaited napkin ring as before (see step 12).

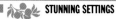 

# Paper Flowers Centrepiece

Choosing tissue paper in closely graded colours for these flowers achieves the vibrant, glowing quality of real live peonies or roses. You can vary the diameter of your paper circles, with 7.5 cm/3 in being about the smallest workable size.

**YOU WILL NEED:** tissue paper in various colours, scissors, florists' wire, darning needle (optional), green crêpe paper.

**1** Cut circles of tissue paper. Fold them into quarters and flute the edges using scissors.

**2** Stack four or six circles of tissue paper together. Bend a small loop in one end of a length of florists' wire. Use a needle to make a hole in the centre of the paper circles, then thread the straight end of the wire through from front to back.

**3** Turn the paper over and gently bunch the circles up around the wire loop. Wind the wire around the base of the flower at the back to secure. Gently ease the tissue paper into attractive 'petal' shapes at the front.

**4** Cut leaf shapes from crêpe paper in proportion to the flower heads. Although crêpe paper is stiffer than tissue, do not make them too large, or they will flop.

**5** Bend small loops at one end of lengths of florists' wire and attach the leaves singly or in pairs. Arrange the finished flowers and leaves in a bowl.

# onbonnières

ese charming lacy holders for candies
sweets are easy to make and look
etty strewn about the table.

**YOU WILL NEED:** for each holder a circle of
tulle or lace about 15 cm/6 in in diameter
plus trimming, needle and thread,

ribbons, sugared almonds, pastel-
coloured mints, cashews, mixed nuts or
other confectionery.

Hem the edge of the fabric circle and trim it
th lace, if you like.

**2** Place a few sugared almonds or other
confectionery in the centre of the circle of
fabric. Tie up the bonbonnière into a neat
bundle with fine satin ribbon. Attach a small
name tag if you like and place the
bonbonnières in position on the table.

# Ribbon Candle Holder Trims

Simple and quick to conjure up, these pretty ribbon trims can be made to echo a special colour scheme. Remember: lit candles should never be left unattended, and make sure they do not burn to within reach of the candle holder trims.

**YOU WILL NEED:** wide-topped candle holders, fine garden or florists' wire, ribbon, scissors, candles, herbs or other greenery (optional).

**1** Wind two or three thicknesses of wire into a ring just large enough to fit neatly inside the top of each candle holder. Twist the ends of the wire around the ring to secure.

**2** Cut the ribbon into pieces about 15 cm/6 in long. Double a length of ribbon and insert the loop under the wire.

**3** Pass the ends of the ribbon through the lo and tighten to knot it on the wire.

**4** Continue knotting ribbon around the wire ring until the wire is completely covered.

**5** Trim the ends of the ribbon to neaten, then repeat for the second ring. Place the wire rings in the candle holders. Decorate with herbs or other greenery if wished.

# lentine's Heart

t hearts a-flutter with this red and white
bon-covered decoration. Choose
bons in pattern variations on your
osen colour scheme. Alternatively, use
tterned and plain fabric, carefully cut
o ribbon strips.

**YOU WILL NEED:** 50–60 cm/20–24 in
thick plastic-covered garden wire, piece
of florists' wire, about 7.5 m/8 yd ribbon
2.5 cm/1 in wide, about 0.5 m/½ yd
ribbon 5 cm/2 in wide, scissors, needle
and thread.

Twist the thick wire into a heart shape and
d the two ends together securely in the
ntre with florists' wire. Cut the narrower
bon into approximately 15 cm/6 in lengths.

**2** Double a length of ribbon and knot it over
the wire. Repeat with more ribbon knots until
the wire is completely covered.

**3** Fold a 20 cm/8 in length of wider ribbon to
make a bow loop and hold it together with a
couple of stitches.

Loop the rest of the wider ribbon around the
ddle of the bow loop and shape into a pair of
ls. Secure with a stitch or two.

Attach the bow at the centre of the heart to
ver the florists' wire. Trim the ends of the
bon into swallowtail shapes.

## Valentine's Day Dinner Party

❖ Cut heart–shaped invitations and
send them to good friends who will
want to share Valentine's Day night
as a foursome.

❖ The menu is light and pink
champagne is the perfect drink!
❖ The idea of the menu is that it can
be romantic for two, or something
of a fun occasion for four. Take the
"pink heart" theme to extremes by

fixing a pink cocktail before dinner
– a mixture of Angostura Bitters,
gin and tonic. It can be fun to go
completely over the top by
preparing heart-shaped cheese
biscuits (crackers) too!

# Woven Heart Bonbon Holder

The symbolic interlacing in this pretty heart-shaped pouch makes it appropriate as a Valentine's Day gift as well as for an engagement announcement. Two colours underline this theme, but the result is attractive when card (posterboard) of just one colour is used.

**YOU WILL NEED:** card, pencil, ruler, scissors, glue, ribbon, shredded tissue paper, bonbons.

**1** Measure and draw a 23 × 15 cm/9 × 6 in oblong shape on two different coloured pieces of card (posterboard).

**2** Cut out the oblongs.

**3** Fold each piece of card in half widthway

**4** Lay the two pieces of card together in an L-shape, with folded sides facing away from you, to form a square where they overlap, and lightly mark in pencil the central point at the top edge where they meet.

**5** Along one short edge of each piece of folded card, measure and mark in pencil two equally spaced 11.5 cm/4½ in lines.

**6** Cut along the marked lines through both layers of card.

**7** Mark smooth curves at each end of the uncut short side of each folded piece of card and cut off the corners to make the rounded top edges of the heart.

**8** Place the two pieces of card side by side, with the folds at right angles to each other and facing outwards. Weave the first strip from the right-hand piece over the nearest strip from the left-hand piece, through the second strip and over the third.

**9** Weave the second strip in the same way the first, alternating the over and under sequence. Weave the third strip in the same way as the first.

Turn the heart over and weave the strips on underside in the same way to make a pouch pe at the top of the heart.

**11** Dab a little glue under the ends of the strips and stick each one down.

**12** Stick lengths of ribbon to the centre back and centre front of the heart, on the inside.

Pack some shredded tissue paper into the art before loosely filling with bonbons.

Tie the ribbons in a bow to close the packet d hold the bonbons inside.

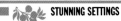
# Silk Posy

The flowers for this posy should include one outstanding 'star', such as a full-blown rose, and a selection of smaller blooms and buds. Leaves and fine composite flower heads provide a delicate background and infilling to the composition.

**YOU WILL NEED:** florists' paper ribbon, silk and/or dried flowers and leaves, fine florists' wire, florists' tape, scissors.

**1** Carefully tear off a narrow strip of ribbon.

**2** Loop the wide length of ribbon once to form a bow shape. Pinch the ribbon together in the centre gently without creasing it too much.

**3** Loop the ribbon again to make a double bow. One end of the ribbon will be in the ce front: loop this end around into a small, ne circle to finish off the bow. Hold it in place the thumb.

**4** Still holding the bow with one hand, thread the narrow strip of ribbon through the central loop of the bow.

**5** Turn the bow over and tie the narrow ribbon firmly to secure the bow. Don't trim the ends.

**6** Attach individual flowers to fine florists' wire. Wire the smaller flowers and buds together in clusters. Tape the wired stems add leaves.

**7** Tie on a strip of ribbon for the tails of the bow. Measure the flowers against the bow when forming the posy. Make the posy alm as wide as the bow at the top, tapering gracefully below. When the shape is right, the flowers together firmly and use the end narrow ribbon to tie them firmly at the back the bow. Make a hanging loop from the nar ribbon, then trim off any excess.

## Pomander Decorations

Orange and lemon pomanders are pretty hung around the kitchen suspended from ribbon, or arranged in a bowl as a table centrepiece. Stud them all over with cloves to keep longer.

**YOU WILL NEED:** oranges and lemons, soft pencil, cloves, ribbon, pins.

**1** Using a soft pencil, lightly mark segments lengthways on the fruit. Press the cloves along the pencilled lines, spacing them evenly.

**2** Take a length of ribbon and wrap it lengthways on the fruit, positioning it between two rows of cloves. Tie it off at one end. Repeat, tying off the second ribbon in the same position as the first.

**3** Take a separate piece of ribbon and thre under the knot of the ribbon on the fruit. Tie into a bow and insert a pin through the ribb and into the fruit to hold it in place. The pin be disguised by folding one loose end of th ribbon over the join and tucking it under.

# bon Rosebuds

y ribbon rosebuds make charming corations for all sorts of occasions, m weddings to christenings. They also ok good as trimmings for table linen and guest rooms.

**YOU WILL NEED:** green and yellow satin ribbon, needle and matching thread, scissors, florists' wire.

**1** Curl the end of a long piece of ribbon into a tight roll.

ecure one end of the roll with a small stitch atching thread.

**3** Make tiny running stitches along the edge of the ribbon to gather it slightly.

**4** Roll the ribbon up, tightly at first and then more loosely until the rosebud is the required size. Trim away surplus ribbon, then turn the raw edge under to prevent fraying and secure with a tiny stitch.

stitch the roses in small clusters to lengths orists' wire.

Jsing green thread, stitch a few loops of en ribbon around the base of the rosebuds. d the ribbon around the wire and secure a stitch.

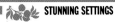
# Wheat Napkin Ring

This simple napkin ring adds a rustic charm to Thanksgiving, harvest suppers or any mealtime occasion when the nights are drawing in.

**YOU WILL NEED:** (for each ring) three small dried leaves, fine florists' wire, paper varnish and brush, three ears of wheat with 25 cm/10 in stems attached, three 25 cm/10 in lengths of stalk without heads, hot water, ribbon.

**1** Wire the stems of the dried leaves.

**2** Paint the leaves with paper varnish and allow to dry.

**3** Soak the wheat stalks for about 30 minut in very hot water to soften them. Drain and blot dry.

**4** Very gently insert a length of florists' wire into each stalk, leaving a little wire protruding at the ends.

**5** Attach a leaf to the base of each wheat ear, then wire in one of the headless stalks.

**6** Plait (braid) the wheat stalks together as evenly as possible.

**7** Twist the plait into a ring and wire in place. Neaten the end.

**8** Tie a ribbon bow below the leaves and wheat ears to conceal the join.

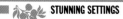 

# Dried-flower Posy

An elegant silk bow is the keynote of this dome-shaped arrangement which makes the perfect adornment for any table. Choose flowers in rich tapestry tones to harmonize with the bow.

**YOU WILL NEED:** silk fabric, needle and matching thread, hemisphere of florists' dry foam (styro foam), florists' wire, about 12 main dried flowers, other smaller flowers and sprays, dried reindeer moss.

**3** Stand back and consider the arrangement before adding final blossoms all around to balance and soften the shape.

**1** Make a large bow of silk fabric and sew a narrow hanging loop to the back. Thread a length of florists' wire through the back of the bow, twist the ends together and stick it into the foam. Begin the arrangement from the bow by inserting some smaller blossoms and moss.

**2** Build up the arrangement around the edges of the foam. Anchor tufts of moss with loops of wire. Distribute the main deep-coloured blooms evenly around the hemisphere. Gradually work in towards the centre, interspersing the main blooms and moss with smaller flowers and sprays.

# olly Table Arrangement

e an attractive bowl or pot as the base
r the arrangement. Poinsettia flowers,
al or silk, make an attractive decoration
the base to cover the gravel.

**YOU WILL NEED:** a length of garden cane
(bamboo stake), a dry florists' foam (styro
foam) sphere, sticky (transparent) tape,
florists' ribbon, scissors, small block of
dry florists' foam, container, gravel,
florists' wire, holly sprigs, artificial
florists' pine sprigs, ivy leaves, real or silk
poinsettias, narrow satin ribbon
(optional), wide decorative ribbon for
container.

**1** Insert one end of a length of garden cane
(bamboo stake) into the foam sphere.

Tape the end of a piece of florists' ribbon to
e top of the cane, then wrap ribbon around
e entire length. Secure with tape at the base.

**3** Insert the end of the garden cane into a
piece of dry foam (styro foam) placed in a
decorative container. Fill with gravel.

**4** Make a loop at one end of a length of
florists' wire and wire individual holly sprigs.
Also wire artificial florists' pine sprigs.

Push the wired stems into the foam to cover
evenly. Add wired individual ivy leaves to fill
y gaps.

Insert the poinsettias into the gravel to
sguise the pebbles. Tie a wide ribbon around
e container. If liked, a few red ribbon bows
an be added to the holly arrangement.

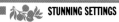 

## Bowl of Candles

Make a bowl of candles for the centrepiece of an informal supper party. Use a bowl which has a lovely rim or highly decorated exterior. Colourful stones or coloured glass pebbles could also be used to cover the sand.

**YOU WILL NEED:** a suitable bowl, sand, coloured candles in different sizes, a range of sea shells.

**1** Fill the bowl two-thirds full with clean sand. The sand must be deep enough to support the candles. Place a tall candle securely in the middle of the bowl.

**2** Place shorter candles around the central candle. Depending on the size of the bowl, you may have room for several rows of candles, with each row getting smaller towards the edge of the bowl.

**3** Once the candles are in position, arrange a variety of pretty shells around them to cover the sand completely.

# nter Candles

s seasonal arrangement of pine cones
d nuts can be transformed into a
ristmas centrepiece with a coating of
d or silver spray paint. Tie a gold or
ver ribbon around the outer rim of the
wl and finish with a bow.

**YOU WILL NEED:** a suitable bowl, sand,
candles of different sizes, pine cones,
selection of nuts.

**NOTE:** Never leave candles unattended
and make sure they do not burn down too
close to any decorative arrangements.

Fill the bowl two-thirds full with clean sand.
e sand must be deep enough to support the
ndles. Place a tall candle in the middle of the
wl, and arrange smaller ones around it.

Once the candles are in position, arrange
he pine cones on the sand.

Fill any gaps left by the pine cones on the
sand with nuts.

# Cocktail Tray

Give a plain or scratched old tray a face-lift with a cut-out paper design. The instructions here show a sophisticated geometric pattern for an oval tray, but the principle can be adapted to any shape of tray. You can trim the tray just to fit it in with a particular party theme, but using strong glue and two coats of clear polyurethane varnish will effect a permanent transformation.

**YOU WILL NEED:** tray, paper for templates, pencil, scissors, ruler, gold and silver good-quality stiff paper, glue, black good-quality stiff paper or tape, paper or polyurethane varnish (optional).

**1** For the first template, take a sheet of paper large enough to cover the base of the tray. Stand the tray on the paper and draw around the base.

**2** Cut out the tray shape. Check that it fits the tray bottom accurately.

**3** Fold the template in half lengthways, then open it out again. Make folds across both ends of the paper as shown, then open them out.

**4** Fold the template in half again along the first fold. Fold the curved ends of the paper back towards the centre, using the second fold as a guide, then pleat the folded ends as shown to make three wedge-shaped creases each end of the template.

**5** Open out the template. Use a ruler and sharp pencil to draw lines along each of the fold marks. Draw the diamond shape and triangles in the middle of the tray. Make a second identical template.

**6** Turn one template over and spread glue evenly on the unmarked side. Stick it down smoothly onto the tray so that the pencil marks are on top.

**7** Fold and then cut the second template in half. You will need this quantity of gold and of silver paper, but do not yet cut out the individual segments.

**8** Mark on both templates which segments are to be gold and which are to be silver: the two colours alternate.

**9** Cut apart the sections of the second template, then cut out the corresponding pieces of gold and silver paper.

**10** Lay the pieces of gold and silver paper in position on the tray, following the marks on the template. Check that they all fit before applying any glue.

Glue the pieces of paper in position on the ⌐y. (The kind of glue depends on how lasting ⌐u want the decoration to be.)

**12** Cut narrow strips of black paper or tape to cover the joins between the different papers. Remember to cut the ends at angles where they join other black strips and to fit the edges of the tray neatly. Carefully glue the strips over the joins.

**13** Coat the finished tray with paper varnish or two coats of clear polyurethane varnish, allowing the varnish to dry thoroughly between coats and before use.

## Decorative Candle Wreath

Highlighted with touches of gold, natural colours and forms glow appealingly in this table centrepiece. Remember that the lit candles should never be left unattended, and make sure they do not burn down to within reach of the wreath.

**YOU WILL NEED:** dry foam (styro foam) ring, four candles, florists' wire, nuts, strong glue, small fir cones, dried hydrangea head, tiny gold baubles, berries or rose hips.

**1** Twist two lengths of wire around the base of each candle, leaving double ends of wire projecting downwards. Spear these wires firmly into the foam ring, spacing the candles evenly.

**2** Stick nuts to the foam in attractive groups.

**3** Add clusters of fir cones between the nu Twist wire around the base of cones that ha no stalks, or use strong glue to stick them place.

**4** Fill spaces in the ring with hydrangea florets (flowerets), sticking them in place with glue. Add baubles and berries as finishing touches.

**NOTE:** Never leave lit candles unattended, and never allow candles to burn down too close to the decorations.

# low and Peach Table
## ntrepiece

en working on a table arrangement to
seen from all sides, it's a good idea to
ep viewing it from different angles to
ke sure that it looks equally good all
nd. This oval arrangement is
mmetrical but evenly balanced.

**YOU WILL NEED:** a container, a block of
wet florists' foam, flowers and foliage
(wired as necessary), ribbon loops.

Establish the overall width and length of the
angement using sprays of leaves as a
ndation. Next place three or five flower
ays at key points to create the outline shape
d height.

**2** Fill in the central shape using clustered
heads of tiny flowers.

**3** Position larger shapely flower heads to add
drama, maintaining the overall shape. Insert
smaller flowers and ribbon bows to finish.

# INDEX

Step-by-step projects are written in *italic*.